W9-BMY-421

22
MUST

PHOTOGRAPHS BY VIGFÚS BIRGISSON
TEXT BY JONAS MOODY

CRYMOGEA

CONTENTS

1. THE BLUE LAGOON

2. ARNARSTAPI

3. FLATEY ISLAND

4. LÁTRABJARG

5. SELÁRDALUR

6. DJÚPAVÍK

7. NÁMASKARÐ

8. ÁSBYRGI

9. DETTIFOSS FALLS

10. ASKJA

11. STÓRURÐ

12. EYSTRAHORN

13. JÖKULSÁRLÓN

14. SVÍNAFELLSJÖKULL

15. LANGISJÓR LAKE

16. LANDMANNALAUGAR

17. DYRHÓLAEY

18. ÞÓRSMÖRK

19. HEIMAEY

20. GULLFOSS

21. GEYSIR

22. ÞINGVELLIR

1

THE BLUE LAGOON

What is it? In the middle of lava field you'll find this spa and hotel utilizing the water from the neighboring geothermal power plant to warm hundreds of thousands of guests every year.

How was it made? In the 1970s, the Suðurnes public electric company built a modern power plant in the Svartsengi geothermal area. The energy is derived from tremendously hot steam tapped through boreholes in the young lava (geologically speaking), which has been permeated by seawater. The seawater collects in large underground pools where it mixes with fresh groundwater to a temperature of 240°C (464°F)—65% seawater, 35% fresh water. This water, called subterranean brine, is extremely rich in minerals and salts, including silica.

What does it do for you? Once the energy was harnessed, there was no use for the subterranean brine so it was dumped into the surrounding lava fields. But then something unexpected happened. As the brine cooled, the silica separated and formed a layer of mud, which slowly began to block the porous lava. This meant water no longer sank into the ground, but instead collected on the surface in a sort of lagoon at the edge of the plant. In 1976, after the plant had been operating for only a couple of months, some of the plant's employees took a dip in the water and discovered this was no ordinary pool. It had therapeutic powers! One of the employees who happened to have psoriasis was surprised that the waters improved his skin condition. Over time, word spread among psoriasis sufferers, and people flocked to the lagoon—both those looking for relief and those seeking a soak in this otherworldly terrain. By then there were calls to have the curative composition of the water examined by experts. In 1999 the Blue Lagoon spa and baths were built and the original lagoon was drained to make room for an extension of the plant.

What makes it so special? After extensive research on the composition of the Blue Lagoon and its effects on the skin, the water's curative powers are now undisputed. These studies have also shown that the microcosm in the lagoon is unlike any other on the planet. For example, microorganisms have been discovered here that exist nowhere else. Although the warm water and number of visitors suggest a prime breeding ground for harmful bacteria, just the opposite is true: it kills bacteria. This is why the Blue Lagoon is not treated with any chemicals.

2

ARNARSTAPI

What is it? A cluster of idyllic houses on Iceland's most stunning harbor girded by a crystal-clear sea, a dazzling, cliff-lined shore and a mystical glacier in the background.

What makes it so special? Arnarstapi's charm is subtle so it may not be apparent at first glance. It's not an actual village, but several houses at the edge of a lava field and mountain chain overlooking the expansive Atlantic Ocean. There still remains a stately aura at Arnarstapi as a reminder of the centuries it was the wealthy estate of a powerful man and an important harbor. In the surroundings, you'll find some of Iceland's most striking natural phenomena, like the Rauðfeldargjá rift opening like a hallway into the mountainside, the mysterious Snæfellsjökull glacier, and the peculiar cliff formations along the coast where the blue ocean water laps at the rock pillars and sea caves. The tiny harbor hidden among the cliffs transports you back to a bygone time of sleepy fishing villages.

What's to see at the bottom of town? Cliffs. The road through Arnarstapi leads down to the harbor. Turn right just before the harbor and follow the coastal road along the ocean. Along the way there's a cave where the roof had been broken through by the sea, so you can look down at the waves and watch the seabirds against the blue-green backdrop. Further south along the shore is the Gatklettur stone arch, which was always a favorite subject among the copperplate etchers who came here on their travels in 18th and 19th centuries. Carry on three kilometers along the coastal nature reserve to the next village, Hellnar, where you'll find more arches and caves. You'll end up at the Hellnar harbor where you'll find one of the country's coziest cafés.

What's next? Visit the mysterious Snæfellsjökull glacier which towers over its peninsula. It was also home to one of Iceland's settlers, Bárður Snæfellsás, who ended his mystic, legendary and incredible life by disappearing inside the glacier. According to the Jules Verne book, Journey to the Center of the Earth, which has twice been made into a film, a crater in the mountain leads down to the Earth's center and comes out the other side at Mount Etna. Regular trips leave from Arnarstapi up Snæfellsjökull on snowcats if you'd rather not trek the glacier by foot.

What should you watch out for? Arctic Terns (*Sterna paradisaea*). Flocks of these birds nest at Arnarstapi. During the nesting season in the summer these kamikaze birds are known to defend their nests fiercely with swooping attacks to the heads of innocent tourists. You can fend them off a number of ways, but it's easiest to just hold a stick in the air.

FLATEY ISLAND

What is it? The island time forgot; in the 19th century it was a flourishing center for commerce and activity.

How do I get there? Flatey is in the middle of Breiðafjörður, the wide fjord above Snæfellsnes peninsula and below the lowest arm of the West Fjords. The ferry Baldur sails across the fjord daily from Stykkishólmur on the Snæfellsnes peninsula to Brjánslækur in the West Fjords, stopping at Flatey along the way. It's possible to send your car ahead and spend more time on the island.

What's there to see? There's no place like Flatey. Nowhere in Iceland can you experience the spirit of a bygone era so richly; the time recreated here evokes one when the Danish-Icelandic culture flourished in tiny timber houses dotting the landscape. Flatey was home to a thriving 19th century commercial hub, but in the 20th century the island's lack of a harbor slowed development until the community was gradually deserted. It was hobbyists who took an interest in restoring the houses and breathed life back into the village, and now nearly every last building has been restored to its original condition. The past is even more prevalent as there are no cars—only old-fashioned tractors used to slowly lug items along the island's only road from the docks to the village. You must take a peek at the church just outside town as well as Iceland's oldest public library, built in the island's heyday in the mid 1800s.

What makes the island remarkable? Just as the island's decline began to hit hardest, Flatey was discovered by artists and became influential in the careers of many of Iceland's writers, visual artists and musicians at the beginning of the 20th century. The church's fresco, by the couple Balthasar and Kristjana Samper, was painted during this prolific period. Later, their son, Balthasar Kormákur, captured Flatey's rustic but enterprising spirit in his film White Night Wedding based on Chekhov's play Ivanov.

What is Flateyjarbók (the Flatey Book)? One of Iceland's greatest national treasures, Flateyjarbók has strong ties to the island. This is the nation's largest and most substantial medieval manuscript, written at the end of the 14th century. It ended up in Flatey's possession for several hundred years. In 1647 a local farmer gave it to the Bishop of Skálholt, who in turn gave it to King Frederick III of Denmark in 1656. Finally, in 1971, the book was returned to Iceland, where it remains in Reykjavík's Culture House.

3

4

LÁTRABJARG

What is it? Europe's largest bird cliff. Icelanders also claim that Bjargtangar, the western end of Látrabjarg, is the westernmost point of Europe, though strictly speaking, the Monchique Islet west of Flores Island in Portugal's Azores archipelago is Europe's westernmost point. However, Icelanders are correct that Látrabjarg is the continent's westernmost point not including remote islands—if that's any consolation.

What's it like? There's a humble, historically preserved lighthouse at Bjargtangar, and if you stand at the lighthouse and look out west over the ocean you'll see ships sailing past, sometimes seals sunning themselves on the rocks, and maybe even a whale spouting. The wind is loud here, but it can't overpower the chorus of thousands of birds below. With such erratic weather, the fear of flying off the cliff's edge keeps most people from stepping too near. However, there are frequent moments of sunshine and calm when the birds glide so close you can almost reach out and touch them. The 14-kilometer stretch of cliff runs east to west, split into several sections by valleys and gulches. Whether it's technically Europe's westernmost point or not, it's well worth a visit.

What birds nest at Látrabjarg? Látrabjarg is a hotspot for razorbills (*Alca torda*). Nowhere in the world are as many razorbills gathered in one place. Actually, nearly half the global population of razorbills converges on Látrabjarg annually. The bird can be recognized by its black head, beak and back, a white breast and a characteristic white stripe down its beak—like a penguin in a mask.

Coastal life. One of the most remarkable features of Icelandic beaches is their black sand. But in the area around Látrabjarg are several light, shell-fragment beaches. For example, the golden sands at Örlygshöfn bay on the way out to Látrabjarg give the shore a far more tropical look than its latitude would suggest. The white sands at Hvallátur directly next to Látrabjarg look like they could have been installed by a Miami landscape artist, although they don't exactly blend in with the lovely old houses and rockpile walls in the vicinity. The largest stretch of golden sand is Rauðisandur east of Látrabjarg, an impressive expanse of shell-fragment sandy beach hugging the southern coast.

5

SELÁRDALUR

What is it? Selárdalur is a remote settlement in a large, majestic fjord, which has been home to a number of "naïve" artists.

What's "naïve" art? Artists are considered "naïve" when they create work in a sophisticated society without conventional training or expertise in their artistic discipline. Their work is born of instinct in the absence of art history and a critical voice. These artists persist with little support or even disapproval from their contemporaries. When Selárdalur farmer Samúel Jónsson (1884-1969) painted a new altarpiece for the parish church the local people declined his offer, claiming the 18th century piece was good enough. So the resolute farmer picked up his tools and with his own two hands built a church—replete with an onion dome—to house his altarpiece. Relying on his own pension, Samúel mixed the cement by hand using sand and gravel from the local beach. An international organization now gathers support to maintain the private church as well as Samúel's other pieces.

Other recluses. Arnarfjörður is undoubtedly one of Iceland's more impressive fjords, flanked by stately mountains and countless valleys. The fjord has long been, and in some ways still is, home to a group of people who march to their own drum. Each valley and farm hides away a man or woman cut from extraordinary cloth, and who come across to outsiders as either inspiring eccentrics or utter conundrums. Some of these recluses are likened to Zen monks in their behavior. Although Elís Kjaran Friðfinnsson may not fit the bill entirely—not actually a native of Arnarfjörður, but rather the fjord to the north, Dýrafjörður—he certainly made his mark on this spectacular corner of the country. In his free time, Elís Kjaran used his tiny bulldozer, dubbed the "Teaspoon", to create a road from Arnarfjörður to a hidden valley called Lokinhamradalur, where two recluses lived on separate farms and never spoke to one another. The road is still passable and should be driven by all who visit the area as a reminder that if you have a bulldozer and enough time, anything is possible.

Hvesta. At the bottom of Arnarfjörður is said to be one of Iceland's most beautiful spots, Hvesta, a golden beach surrounded by the towering figures of Arnarfjörður's mountains. There is talk of building an oil refinery on this site, so hurry up and get a few pictures before it's too late!

DJÚPAVÍK

What is it? A tiny village accessible only via a winding road through one of Iceland's most remote areas.

Why go there? In Djúpavík, visitors to the country can see how life on the island used to be. The road along the Strandir coast threads through deep fjords and cuts across steep mountainsides as a lifeline for the few inhabitants left in this corner of the world. Djúpavík is one of the more picturesque places in the area. Originally a factory village at the base of high cliffs and a roaring waterfall, the settlement wasn't even accessible by road during its heyday in the 1930s and '40s. Life revolved around herring then, and once the herring stocks disappeared from the nearby fishing grounds, the people moved away, leaving behind a ghost town. In 1985, however, a section of the old factory shops was converted into a hotel, and people started living permanently in the village once again.

Where do you go from there? Djúpavík is on the south shore of Reykjarfjörður fjord. There is a deserted village, Gjögur, on the north shore, and in the next fjord, Norðurfjörður, is yet another village. All these places were once much larger, but are now quickly fading into oblivion, having outlived their usefulness to the life of the nation. There is an undeniable sense of calm in these quiet villages, echoed in the hills and seaside, where even the babbling mountain streams can be heard.

What's the story behind the factory? The first buildings at Djúpavík were erected shortly after WWI. In 1935, a factory was built in record time as well as several surrounding buildings. At that time, the ship was hauled up on land (where it remains today, almost entirely rusted) to serve as housing for the construction workers. The entire village was operated by the factory, including a bakery, a store and a large cafeteria for the workers. In its day, the factory was one of the largest buildings in Iceland and housed cutting-edge equipment.

Don't miss this. As you head north into Norðurfjörður fjord the road ends at a warm pool at Krossnes, with the Arctic Ocean to one side and a mountain to the other. A dip in the pool is the icing on the cake at the end of this trip along the Strandir coast.

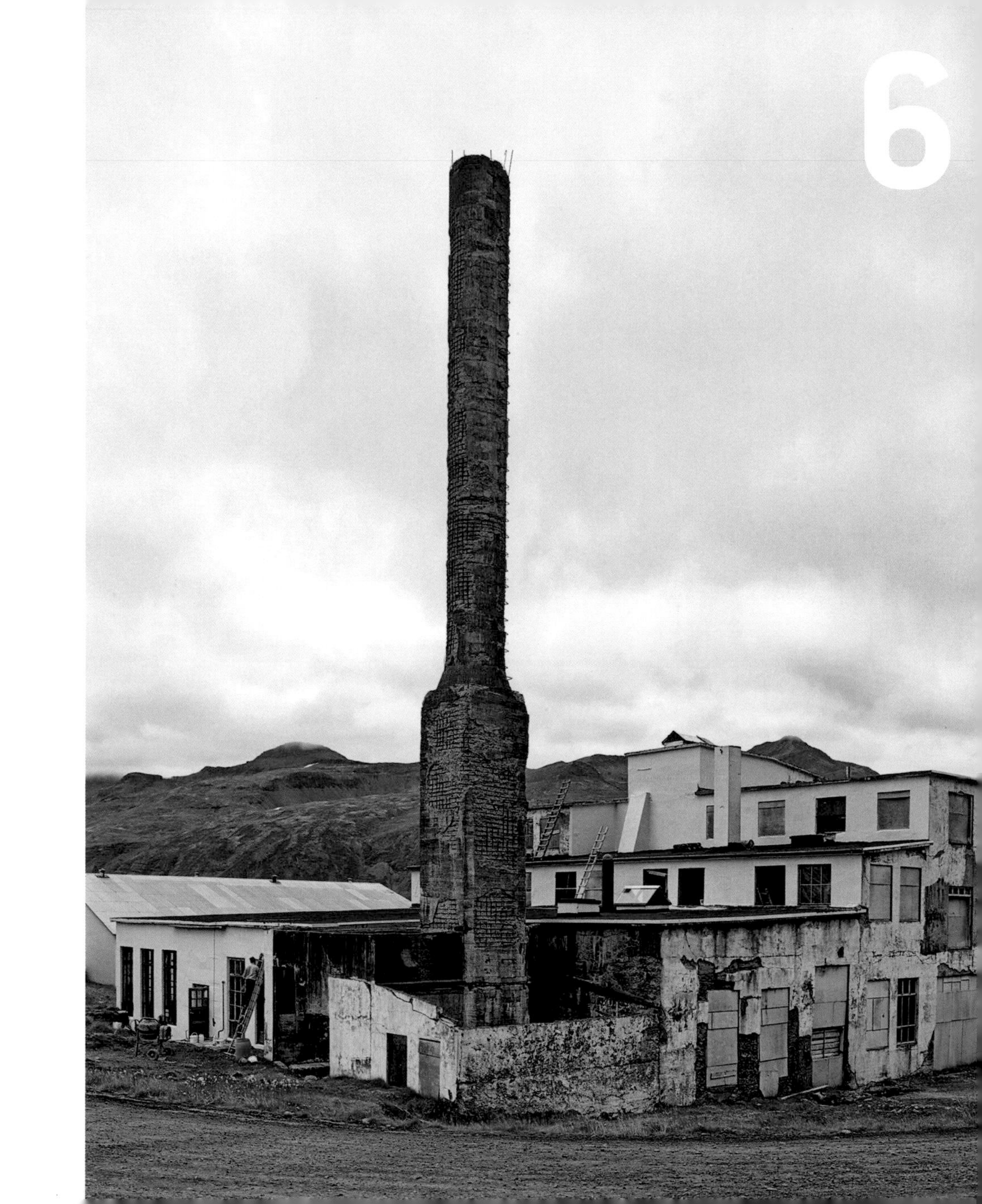
6

7

NÁMASKARÐ

What is it? Very large and accessible geothermal area, known for its boiling mud pots. Part of the Mývatn area, one of Iceland's most spectacular areas for natural phenomena.

What's to see? On the roadside of Route 1, the Námaskarð geothermal area is divided into two sections: the boiling mud pots on level ground and Mount Námafjall above. Most people only see the mud pots, as they are well marked and easily accessible from a wooden walkway. But the hiking path up the mountain is stunning as well. Bathed in the glowing reflection of the sulfurous rock, with steaming fumaroles at every step, the hike is almost otherworldly. The mountainside is steep, but low with a path clearly separated from the mud pots by posts.

Hot as hell! The Mývatn area lies along the rift between the North American and Eurasian continental plates. For this reason, geothermal activity abounds at every turn: lava fields, craters, hot springs, steam and sulfur. There are other geothermal areas nearby which you can find if you take the road north from Námaskarð, past the geothermal power plant and on to a parking lot for Leirhnjúkur crater. Over the course of a short walk, you'll see boiling mud pots and lava fields dating back to different geological periods, as well as the remnants of an eighteenth century eruption and the Krafla fires, a series of volcanic events which took place from 1975 to 1984. The Krafla area includes the explosion crater Víti (literally "hell"), formed in a 1724 eruption. At the bottom of the crater is lime-green lake made even brighter by its ochre surroundings. Nearby is a small canyon full of sulfurous deposits and boiling mud pots.

Don't miss Lake Mývatn. On the other side of Mount Námafjall is Lake Mývatn, a backdrop to a host of natural wonders like countless lava formations and pseudocraters, which are formed when molten lava meets water. Many find it a remarkable place as it's also the home of numerous duck species that live off the local gnats (or in Icelandic "mý", from where the lake draws its name), insects which surround the lake in such large swarms that the air can appear black.

8

ÁSBYRGI

What is it? A canyon with cliff walls rising 100 meters over its flat, wooded bottom.

How was it formed? Ásbyrgi is part of Vatnajökull National Park, and, like the adjacent Jökulsárgljúfur canyons, was formed by the Jökulsá á Fjöllum river. Since the end of the last ice age about 10,000 years ago, the river has run into the sea on its current path. However, Vatnajökull, the glacier that feeds the river, has been affected by the changing climates, sometimes retreating so far that it only remained on the mountain peaks, and sometimes growing and spreading out. Today Vatnajökull covers about 8000 square kilometers. Under the glacier are some of Iceland's most active volcanoes, which may suddenly erupt and cause serious flooding. The same can happen when the glacier shifts or spreads out. Large ice dams create huge lagoons. When these break, a tidal wave is released, which, under the right conditions, can wipe out the ground in an instant. Because of the volume of water and the tremendous pressure, the water can force itself into underground vacuums and crevices in the rock and shatter it. As the larger pieces succumb, the rupture grows until entire cliffs topple under the water's might. It's thought that such tidal waves have washed over the land since the last ice age—the last about 2000 years ago. It was one such catastrophic flood that formed Ásbyrgi.

The Myth. It's often said that the horseshoe-shaped Ásbyrgi is the hoof print of Sleipnir, the eight-legged steed of Odin, king of the gods at Valhöll. On one of Odin's rides, Sleipnir accidently flung one of his eight hooves into the rock, forming Ásbyrgi. Some say the proof is Eyjan, the single stand of cliffs in the middle of the canyon, where the center of the hoof struck. This story, however, is a latter day invention from a romantic poet who visited the site and saw the landscape as a symbol of mythical power. The poet, Einar Benediktsson, was so drawn to Ásbyrgi that he bought the plot and owned it for some time.

What's there to see? Everyone who visits Ásbyrgi should climb up Eyjan, "The Island", a single stand of cliffs in the middle of the canyon. There's an easy and well-marked hiking path heading north from the camping ground. The top of Eyjan provides a good vantage point to appreciate fully the scope of this massive wonder and the awesome power it must have taken to form it. It's also worth your time to hike to the pond and spring at the bottom of Ásbyrgi. The cliffs are highest here, creating the feeling of standing in a huge ravine. It's a delightful spot to spend an early summer morning.

9

DETTIFOSS FALLS

What is it? One of Europe's most powerful waterfalls, where the Jökulsá á Fjöllum river falls some 44 meters into a wide canyon. The rust-colored water carries sediment from its source in Vatnajökull, Europe's largest glacier. The rough-hewn cliffs and thunderous roar leave a lasting impression on visitors.

How do I get there? You can approach the falls from east or west of the river. The road that heads to the east bank has for years been considered the worst road in Iceland and, well into the early spring, is often impassable due to mud slicks and snow. There is a new paved road on the west bank which allows easy access for all kinds of vehicles during the summer months. The road will continue to Ásbyrgi in the near future. From both parking lots on the west and east sides there is a short, well marked hike to the falls. From the east there is a spectacular view of the canyons the river has carved out as well as mist from the next waterfall below, Hafragilsfoss. It's best to approach from the west where the road leads down to the falls. Anyone who visits the national park will tell you it's most striking to approach Hafragilsfoss from down in the canyons.

What else is in the area? The Jökulsárgljúfur canyons, including Dettifoss, are part of Jökulsárgljúfur National Park. The canyons include a number of cliff formations well worth a look. Close to the park visitors' center, Gljúfrastofa, is Tröllahellir cave at the river, and just beyond are the "men in the cliffs", Karl and Kerling. Still more impressive are the Hljóðaklettar bluffs to the north. These are the core of an old crater row after the Jökulsá river washed away the overlying sediment. The southernmost cliff, nicknamed "the lion's head", greets visitors to the bluffs who arrive from the visitors' center. The road then leads to the great Álfakirkja "Elf Church", which is a triangular cave with a ceiling of columnar basalt.

The Python's Gaze. Dettifoss was unknown to visitors to Iceland before the mid 19th century. The Englishman Rev. Sabine Baring-Gould (1834-1924) believed he was the first to "discover" the falls on his trip to Iceland in 1861, recording his adventure in his book *Iceland: Its Scenes and Sagas* from 1863. Icelandic writers in the latter half of the 19th century were greatly drawn to the waterfall, seeing it as a symbol of nature's majesty, the force of progress or even their own death wish. All these men described the waterfall's effect, the way it compelled them to draw nearer. Many who visit the falls today can sense its "python's gaze".

10

ASKJA

What is it? A volcano, though now the crater is filled with a lake called Öskjuvatn, creating a barren and ominous landscape. Beside Askja is a smaller crater lake, which, despite the slightly disconcerting name of Víti ("Hell"), is a delightful geothermal pool for skinny-dipping: you won't get hauled in for public indecency and don't have to pay a single penny for admission. The crater bottom is shielded from highland winds, so on good days you can sunbathe on the lakeside and warm up every now and then in the silica-rich, sulfurous water. A dip in "Hell" in really something everyone should try.

Is there a trail around the water? The crater walls are all rather steep and in some places nearly vertical. It's possible to go around the lake, but not along the shore, and it takes much longer than most think—an entire day. For a different landscape take the posted trail from the Dreki mountain hut in Drekagil ravine over the Dyngjufjöll mountains to the lake. The route takes you through a landscape covered in pumice, and although it's uphill the hike is not too difficult. The hike reaches its summit up the mountain pass when you look out over Öskjuvatn lake. The entire area has an awesome, electric aura about it, which is somehow more prominent from this perch.

How do I get there? Askja is in the highlands, meaning you need a specially equipped vehicle to ford some of the rivers along the way. You can't drive all the way to the lake as the road ends at the parking lot near the newest lava field, which was formed in an eruption in 1961.

Is it possible to sail on Öskjuvatn? There aren't any trips on the lake as there are no boats in the vicinity. There's actually no one patrolling the area and no tourist services of any kind, since the place is so far off the beaten path. But it's a truly and spectacular place in all its unspoiled emptiness. The lake was formed after Askja's last large eruption in 1875, which also formed Víti. Öskjuvatn is Iceland's deepest lake at a depth of 220 meters.

11

STÓRURÐ

What is it? A massive stand of rocks rising out of a blue-green lake on one of Iceland's most picturesque mountains.

How do I get there? Stórurð was almost unheard of until 1970 when some clever locals pointed out that north of the Dyrfjöll mountains was one of the more remarkable sites in Iceland. Yet guidebooks are still published with no mention of the place. Stórurð can only be reached by foot, and you should figure on at least half a day's hike based on the shortest route. There are four paths to Stórurð, and you should stick to them. The East of Iceland is known for its blitz fog that drops out of nowhere, so it's good to follow a marked path. The Dyrfjöll mountains are impressive, forming the boundary between Fljótsdalshérað county and Borgarfjörður Eystri. The mountains can be seen from far away, and it doesn't take long to realize where they get their name, Dyr-fjöll ("Door-mountains"), from the large gap in their profile. It's a door in the mountainside carved away by millennia of glacial erosion, leaving the gap quite even. The western path to Stórurð comes in from the road to Borgarfjörður eystri fjord while the eastern path begins in the village of Borgarfjörður eystri. The path from Vatnsskarð on the road (at the top of it) is the simplest and most direct, but for those who want to experience the lovely Borgarfjörður eystri fjord, the path begins at the village of Bakkafjörður.

What's there to see at Stórurð? There are three parts to appreciating Stórurð. Firstly, as the site is in the Dyrfjöll mountains, the proximity to the summits and the "door" is impressive on its own. Secondly, Stórurð is made up of unusual rocks, like a pile of Stonehenge megaliths or stones from the ruins of a great palace. But there's nothing supernatural about their presence. The glacier that once covered the mountain carved the stones from the cliffs and carried them along as it crept out. When the ice melted, the stones were deposited. Last but not least, you'll see the ponds between the stones: their sea-blue color becomes ethereal in the fog when the water seems to glow with beams of light.

12

EYSTRAHORN

What is it? A mountain, but not for climbing—only for admiring.

What's there to admire? Standing in the southeast corner of the country, Eystrahorn is a reflection of its nearby twin, Vesturhorn. Both mountains stand at the end of a curved fjord. At the mouth of the fjord is a brackish lagoon fed from mountain streams and run-off water from Vatnajökull glacier. The lagoon is girded from the sea by a long sandbar and closed off by the surrounding mountains. Originally the road through the area led through a high, steep pass into Hornafjörður fjord to the south and a treacherous plateau to the north, but a tunnel and roads cutting through the scree have since replaced the more hazardous route. Route 1 lies at the foot of Eystrahorn, so you can see it from your car as you drive by. However, for a proper look, pull off the road towards the orange Hvalnessviti lighthouse at the end of the headland beside the mountain. Here you can step out of your car to admire the mountain in the fullness of the sea and the scree surrounding it, and perhaps take a short jaunt along the shore if time allows.

What about hiking it? You can't hike up the front of the mountain, up the scree and onto the summit, without climbing gear. But with permission from Hvalsnes farm, picturesquely located just under the mountain, you can hike in through the "backdoor" of the mountain from the lighthouse parking lot up the slope. You won't be able to crest the mountain, but you'll be able to see the surroundings ever better.

What's next? Behind the farms scattered throughout Lón, the area around the lagoon, and really any farms in the southlands, stands the mighty Vatnajökull glacier. The glacial and volcanic
activity of the past millennia has carved a unique landscape above Lón known as Lónsöræfi. What characterizes Lónsöræfi is its landscape of colorful rock formations, numerous ravines and steep mountains against the backdrop of Vatnajökull glacier. Lónsöræfi boasts one of the highland's favorite hiking paths, from Mount Snæfell, over Brúarjökull glacier and finally down into Lónsöræfi itself. For a peek into the area take one of the organized daytrips. This gets you over the rivers and rough roads by bus or car. You can sign up for a trip in the nearby village of Höfn í Hornafirði.

13

JÖKULSÁRLÓN

What is it? A glacial lagoon: ice floes and icebergs floating on a lake with a glacier and mountains in the background. One of the nation's most treasured sites.

When was it discovered? The glacial lagoon at Breiðamerkursandur didn't exist at the beginning of the 20th century. As it began to form very few people knew of its existence besides the people in the immediate area, as this was once one of the country's most remote places. There were no bridges over the glacial rivers that flank Öræfasveit, the area between the glacial lagoon, and Skeiðará river, until 1967 when the current suspension bridge was erected at the bottom of the lagoon. However, it wasn't until 1974 that the rivers cutting across the Skeiðarársandur drainage basin were bridged entirely. This was the final phase of the ring road around Iceland, meaning people could suddenly drive from Reykjavík to Jökulsárlón in under a day. The lagoon fast became a major tourist destination in the 1980s and is now one of the most photographed sites in the country. The lagoon also served as a backdrop for James Bond films including A View to a Kill and Die Another Die as well as Tomb Raider and Batman Begins.

How was it formed? An extension of the Vatnajökull glacier, the Breiðamerkurjökull glacier slid forward in the 17th, 18th and 19th centuries until there were only a couple hundred of meters between it and the shoreline. The huge amounts of glacial run-off water during this time formed the Jökulsá river in Breiðamerkursandur, which was considered a terrible obstacle to transportation; essentially it was brown water gushing out from under the glacier and ripping through the terrain before flowing out to sea. During this time people and horses had to trek across the cracked, slippery ice to reach the other side. But in the 20th century the glacier receded and the river forked with a lagoon forming at the eastern estuary in 1930. In 1935, a lagoon formed at the western estuary, and in 1944 the two lagoons merged. Jökulsárlón continues to grow, and it recently came to light that the lagoon is actually a 200-300 meter-deep fjord carved out by the glacier. Strangely enough, the lagoon is privately owned. So hypothetically, it's possible to buy it.

What's there to do? Go out on the water. It's the only way to properly see this bizarre, constantly changing natural wonder. Since the ice melts and drifts and new icebergs drop into the water, the lagoon never looks the same from one day to the next. This is a true wonderland, one that can be appreciated only to a small degree from land.

14

SVÍNAFELLSJÖKULL

What is it? A glacial icefall just under Hvannadalshnúkur, Iceland's highest peak, Svínafellsjökull tumbles down an awesome and beautiful valley. You can drive right up to it.

See for yourself. Vatnajökull glacier and its surroundings were made into a national park in 2008. This is Europe's largest national park, although it's almost entirely covered in ice. One of the most accessible and impressive portions of the national park is the area at Skaftafell. There's no other area in the Vatnajökull area as visitor-friendly with such well-marked paths where you'll see all sorts of glacial formations and the terrain they have carved out. Also, there's no other icefall as easily accessible in Iceland as Svínafellsjökull. It only takes a moment to reach the icefall from the highway turnoff winding through the tall glacial "waves", which are what's left from the glacier's slide forward during a colder era. However, like most glaciers during the current era, the ice is retreating. Bear in mind that the parking lot and road to Svinafellsjökull were entirely covered in ice until 1940, and that Svínfellsjökull and Skaftafellsjökull to the west formed a single icefall at that time.

Hiking the glacier. The tourist center at Skaftafell serves as the center for glacier trips in the area. If you'd like to hike up on Svínafellsjökull and experience what it's like to charge across a crevassed icefall in constant (albeit extremely slow) movement, then you can get instructions here as well as the necessary equipment for hiking the glacier. You can also follow the edge of the glacier along the valley wall to see how the ice has scraped away the rock and vegetation so all that's left is crumbled stone. If you choose not to go out on the ice then this hike is also rewarding, since the landscape is truly remarkable.

Global warming. The icefalls in the Skaftafell area are currently receding quickly, which is a consequence of higher average temperatures. Stop for a moment where the glacier abuts a little pond and listen. You'll hear the mesmerizing murmur of a millions little drops falling from the ice. This is the tragic sound of global warming. Several years ago a British artist set up a microphone and a mobile phone connection to broadcast the sound to her gallery in London, with the express purpose of engaging people's senses in global changes.

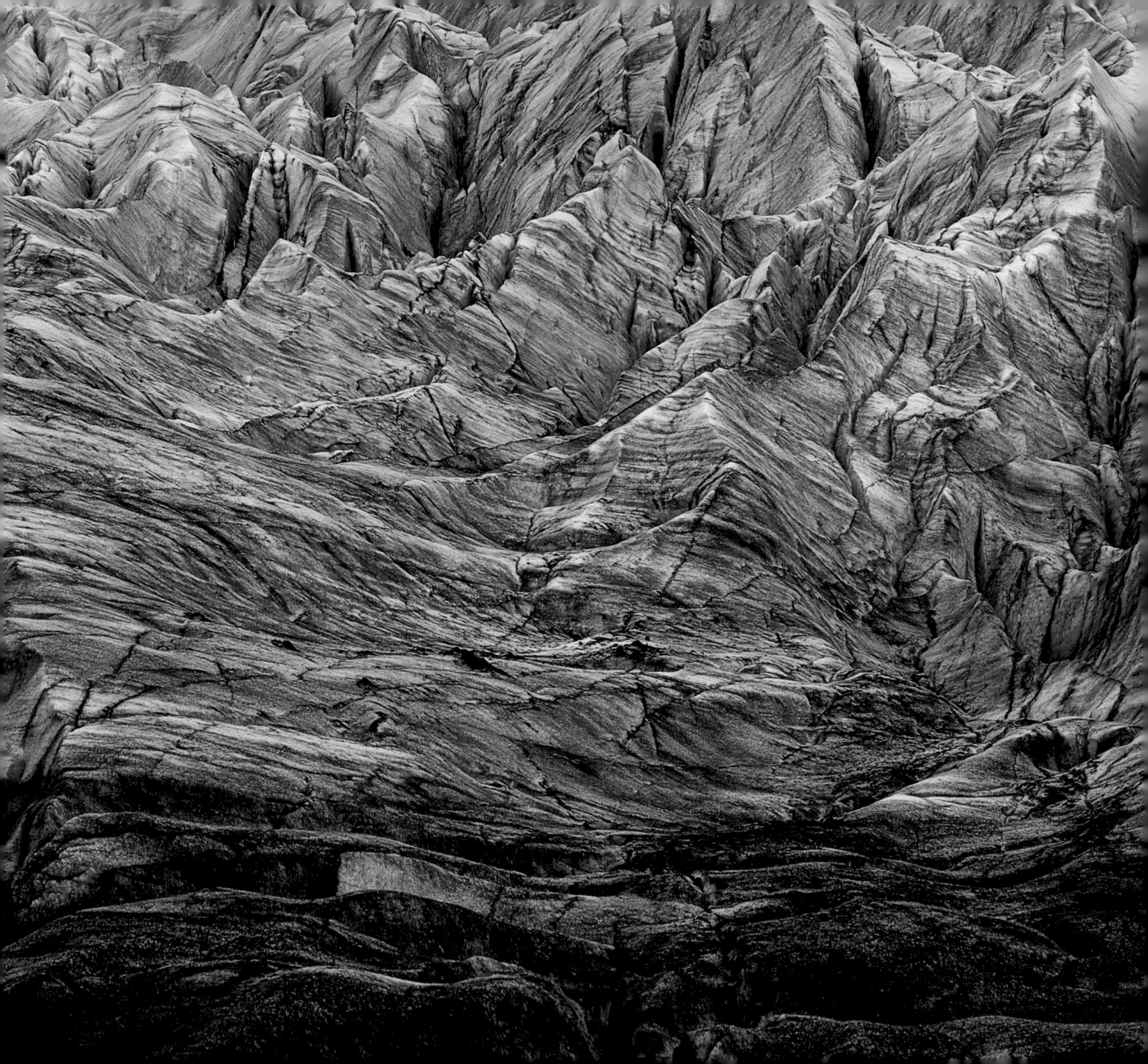

15

LANGISJÓR LAKE

What is it? A clear, blue highland lake set in a black sandy wasteland flanked by mountains with a glacier in the background.

How do you get there? Langisjór is only accessibly by 4x4 or mountain bus or on foot, meaning there's relatively little traffic around the lake considering this is absolutely one of Iceland's most impressive sites. A road from the southwest leads to the lake, where the road ends. From there you'll need to travel on foot. There is a trodden hiking path on the lake's southeastern shore along the Fögrufjöll mountains, which seperate Langisjór and the Skaftá river basin. There are signs posted along the way to keep you on the right track. It's not recommended that you strike out on these paths without the right hiking equipment as you are a long way from civiliation. Give yourself ample time to hike the ring around the lake—three to four days. If you have the time, you won't be sorry. The same it true of those who can only stop for the day to hike along the shore next to the Fögrufjöll mountains.

The discovery of the lake. There are no records of travels to Langisjór before 1854. In fact, it was not named until 1890 when explorer Þorvaldur Thoroddsen dubbed it Langisjór, the "Long Sea". The extent of the lake's outflow wasn't uncovered until 1940, and the first map to show its entire shape wasn't printed until 1950. Langisjór was a glacial lagoon, murky with silt, into the 20th century, but when the glacier receded the water took on the clear, blue color it has today. Langisjór wasn't recognized as an interesting natural phenomenon until later in the 20th century. Until then there were plans to use it as a reservoir for power plants, which would have meant the lovely blue water would have once again turned grey and murky.

What's it like at the lake? Many people describe visiting the lake as a religious experience. A hike around the water certainly does leave a lasting impression, both because of how few people visit the lake and how its long, narrow shape resembles a kind of inland fjord girded by mountains. The walk brings you ever closer to the glacier north of the lake, and when the sun shines the white cap glows in the distance like heaven itself. The Fögrufjöll mountains are also striking, with their long ridge punctuated with mountain lakes. If you hike up the mountainside you'll be rewarded with views of the Skaftá river basin and further south to the Lakagígur craters and the Veiðivötn cluster of lakes. With a vast expanse of untamed glacial rivers and lava fields in one direction, and azure waters and the broad Vatnajökull glacier in the other, this is as close as you can get to the essence of Icelandic nature.

16

LANDMANNALAUGAR

What is it? Natural pools in the highlands and the hub for the surrounding wonderland of colorful mountains, lava formations and canyons.

How do you get there? Landmannalaugar is one of the most popular destinations in the highlands. However, like most spots in the highlands, it isn't exactly accessible by road except in the summer (not counting winter jeep trips), and even then only by 4x4 or mountain bus. Landmannalaugar is the starting block and finish line for the highland's hottest hike, Laugavegur, which leads from Skógar or Þórsmörk to Landmannalaugar, depending on whether you take the longer or shorter route. Hikers approaching from the south (from Skógar or Þórsmörk) are in for a treat when they reach their destination; a dip in the springs is a huge carrot at the end of a hard day of trekking. The pool is fed by a mix of cold and hot springs, creating water just right for a relaxing soak.

What's there to see? – First impressions. Most visitors who come for a short stop at Landmannalaugar hike up Bláhnúkur peak (945 meters), as it's close to the pool. A marked and heavily trafficked path leads up the mountain along a steep ridge, although it's not too difficult for experienced hikers.

What's there to see? – The next level. To fully experience the magic of this region, take a walk up Brennisteinsalda. This moderate hike affords some spectacular views of the glorious colors that put this place on the map. The electric green moss and glowing yellow of the sulfur mixes with the greens, browns, blues and yellows of the rhyolite rock. Set against the black Laugahraun obsidian, this kaleidoscope of color becomes nearly dizzying. Adding to this diverse landscape are views of the complex system of canyons carved out by the rivers and lakes in the area. If you want to see nature's capacity for dazzling color, then Brennisteinsalda is the right place.

What's there to see? – Worth the effort. The entirety of Landmannalaugar has been formed by rhyolite, geothermal heat, snow and water. But nowhere is the interaction among natural erosion, geothermal heat and volcanic activity as overwhelming as at Jökulgil canyon. The canyon stretches out before the parking lot at Landmannalaugar including views of Mount Austurbarmur along the canyon with its stunning, light-colored screes. Hiking into the canyon is no walk in the park, wading through glacial streams over and over through the uneven terrain of the canyon floor.

17

DYRHÓLAEY

What is it? A huge stone arch surrounded by black sand that extends out into the Atlantic Ocean.

What's there to see? Dyrhólaey is a nature preserve, so the entire area – or parts of it – is sometimes closed during the spring nesting season. But outside those times it's a great experience to visit the southernmost point of the island. As if standing on the prow of ship, you can look south over the Atlantic Ocean knowing there is no land ahead until the South Pole. On bright days the horizon seems to recede, and you can see the tops of waves out into the point of infinity. Flanking the site, the black beach of the Southlands stretches out along the coast. The next glacial river to the west, Jökulsá á Sólheimasandi, dumps a continuous flow of black grit into the sea, contending with the water to overtake Dyrhólaey. The sand works to envelope the rock while the sea competes to return it to its original form—the arch is thought to have been formed as part of an underwater eruption at the end of the last ice age when the sea level was higher.

What else is there to do? Dyrhólaey is a picturesque spot, both looking up from the beach and looking down from atop the rock. Kill two birds with one stone and head down to the Reynisfjara beach at the base of Mount Reynisfjall east of Dyrhólaey. There you'll find Reynisdrangar, a series of majestic stone stacks in the sea, as well as a grotto in the rock accessible at low tide, but watch out for the cave to fill up with the incoming tide. If there's enough time, the walk down the black beach to Dyrhólaey is impressive, especially if there are large waves breaking and the sea is choppy. However, one should bear in mind that the southern coast faces the Atlantic Ocean directly, and people have been known to drown when chasing waves out to sea. The waves are much larger and more powerful than they appear, and the undertow is deceptively strong. There are a number of incidents every year, so be careful.

Portland. For centuries English sailors fished the waters south of Iceland. They were familiar with Dyrhólaey and called it "Portland". The outermost part of the rock sticking out into the sea is called Tóin, and you can cross it to get out to the section of the rock in the sea. It's relatively easy to sail through the archway if the conditions are right and this is often done. Flying through it, however, is more challenging. In 1985 two Icelandic hotshots were the first to make it through.

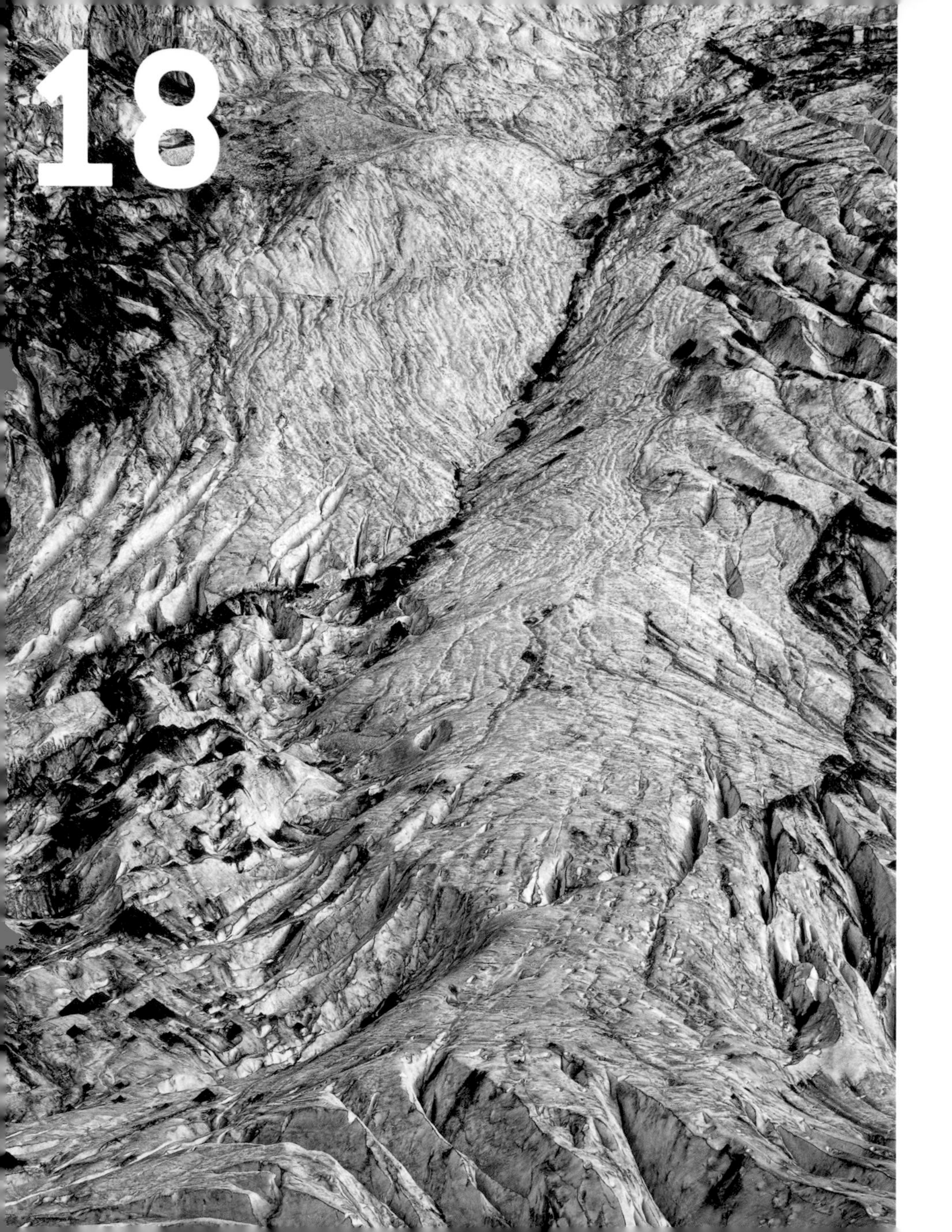
18

ÞÓRSMÖRK

What is it? A wilderness reserve acting as the hub for some of the country's most popular hiking paths known for its glacial vistas, powerful rivers, birch groves and large fissures.

What's the area like? Þórsmörk is not too deep into the wilderness, just a short distance from Route 1, but still very much in the highlands. For example, the outpost at Húsadalur is not actually accessible by road as on the way one most ford the Krossá, a powerful glacial river which is perilous to cross, as many off-roaders have discovered (the hard way). Hikers, however, have it better off with a small, but trusty, footbridge over the mighty Krossá. Most hikers cross directly over Þórsmörk, either heading from Skógar in the south and further north from Landmannalaugar or back down on the so-called Laugavegur path (not to be confused with Reykjavík's main drag!). There are three spots to stay in Þórsmörk: Húsadalur, Langidalur and Básar, and you'll have no problem getting there as frequent organized trips service the area.

What's there to do? Þórsmörk presents a powerful experience, especially with the views of the glacier. The Eyjafjallajökull glacier dominates the views to the south and west while to the east you'll see an icefall from Mýrdalsjökull glacier. The small Tindfjallajökull glacier can also be seen to the northwest. The entire area abounds with marked hiking paths, and at all three of the site's outposts are park staffers whom hikers can consult on the best routes and what to see. Although many hard-core hikers see Þórsmörk as a mere stopover on the way to Landmannalaugar, you don't have to look hard to realize the awesome beauty of this place: a striking mix of stark, raw landscapes alongside more bucolic meadows alive with birch trees and wildflowers.

Ash trouble. The Eyjafjallajökull glacier sits over an active volcano, but as it had been dormant since the early 19th century, the infamous 2010 eruption came as a surprise to all but the geologists monitoring its activity. The initial eruption in March began on the hiking trail from Skógar to Þórsmörk. With little ash and plenty of spewing lava, this photogenic event attracted many tourists, but became only the prelude to a much more powerful outbreak in the ice-filled crater of Eyjafjallajökull just a few weeks later. The flood of mud and water from the crater left the local inhabitants unharmed but the giant ash cloud that rose to the skies caused havoc for tens of millions of air travelers worldwide when European air space was closed for days. The eruption itself lasted only a few weeks – a mere instant in global terms – but the unpronounceable name of Eyjafjallajökull still has the power to make people cringe.

19

HEIMAEY

What is it? The most densely populated island around Iceland, where an eruption from 1973 buried the village under lava and ash. Many islanders returned after the calamity to rebuild their home.

Why is it remarkable? Heimaey is part of the Westman Islands, an archipelago known for its volcanic activity. In 1963 there was an underwater eruption off Heimaey's southern coast, and when the eruptions stopped fours years later a new island had risen from the sea named Surtsey after the fire giant from Norse mythology. Surtsey is a unique living laboratory for biology and geology to study how terrain is formed and life develops on new land, which is why it's listed as a UNESCO World Heritage site. No one may set foot on the island but researchers. Later, on January 23, 1973, it was Heimaey's turn. The eruption began in the middle of the night, but all 6,000 islanders were miraculously evacuated to the mainland. When the eruption finally ended that July, the lava had enlarged the island considerably but also buried half the village.

What's there to do? Heimaey presents a diverse landscape considering its size. The large bluffs on the northern side of the island are one piece of this mosaic. It's relatively easy to access them from the harbor, but don't climb up the eastern bluff, Heimaklettur, unless you're with a local. Another piece is the volcano that formed in 1973, Eldfell. The ground is still warm here, and it's a good place to get an idea of past volcanic eruptions and the new layers of lava. The next piece is Cape Stórhöfði on the southern coast where you can take in the other Westman Islands. For the complete show take a boat out around the island, as it's the only way to access the Heimaklettur sea caves, truly one of the island's wonders.

Þjóðhátíð – The Nation's Festival. The first weekend in August the Westman Islanders throw the biggest village shindig of the year called Þjóðhátíð, where vast numbers of Icelanders from all around the country descend on tiny Heimaey. The festival was first held in 1874 when Iceland got its first constitution. These days the festival is set up in a natural amphitheater just outside town where the locals celebrate in large, white tents. If you're looking to sing, drink and make merry with the islanders, this is your chance.

20

GULLFOSS

What is it? Iceland's most famous waterfall.

What's there to see? Gullfoss has been one of the most frequented tourist sites in Iceland since the 18th century. Its allure lies in the sheer magnitude of the water and height of the falls, which is made up of two segments. The upper cascade is smaller, while the lower cascade is quite deep. The water tumbles down a sort of rocky stairway between the canyon walls until it plunges deep into the rock, which can't be seen unless you stand at the edge of the waterfall. The fall doesn't reveal itself all at once. Approaching from the top all you see are the rapids, which don't suggest a very exciting waterfall. But as you approach and the roar of the water falling into the canyon grows, you realize its enormity. But it's not until you stand at the edge of the canyon peering down into its depths that you see the full extent of the lower segment. Because you approach the top of the waterfall at ground level, the vantage point and accessibility are excellent. The grassy slopes around the canyon create a gentler beauty alongside the stunning power in front of you. As you edge out towards the canyon to see the lower segment and the water falling into the canyon, Gullfoss finally reveals itself in the fullest as the water hurls down a long narrow chute in the rock. As always, when the full power is revealed in stages instead of all at once, the effect is even more dazzling. Gullfoss leaves a lasting impression.

The Golden Circle. It's not far from Geysir to Gullfoss. These two sites, the hot spring and the waterfall, have been partnered since tourists and scientists first began coming to Iceland in search of adventure. In the 20th century the trip to these sites along with Þingvellir got the name "The Golden Circle" as most of Iceland's major natural wonders were seen in a single day trip.

Emblem of nature conservation. Around 1900 there were plans to build a power plant at Gullfoss, but for a number of reasons the plant was never built. The best known reason is the intervention of Sigríður from Brattholt, a farmer's daughter from a nearby farm. Sigríður fought for the waterfall's preservation, and thereby made Gullfoss an emblem of nature conservation in Iceland.

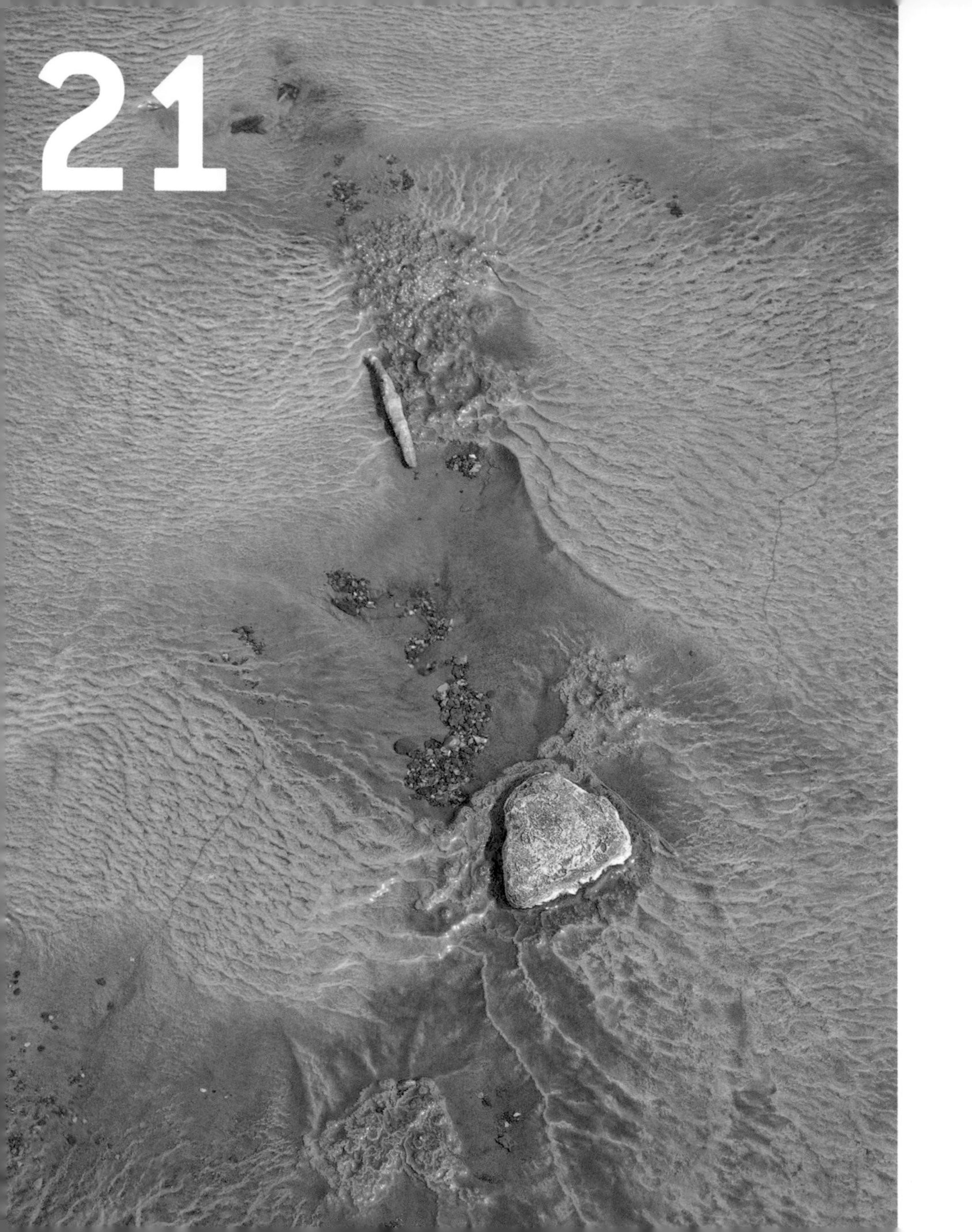
21

GEYSIR

What is it? Iceland's most famous geyser (and the namesake of all geysers). After years of dormancy, the spring was reawakened by an earthquake in 2000, and now spouts off every now and then. If you miss Geysir, then you'll be sure to catch his little brother, Strokkur, which erupts at regular intervals all year like clockwork.

Why do geysers erupt? Long story, short: water boils, changes into steam and surges up to the surface. Short story, long: water in the springs is heated to the boiling point, which causes it to expand. But the water must overcome its surface tension to form bubbles, which is why a dormant geyser can be made to erupt by pouring soap into it, as was often done in the past. The soap lowers the water's surface tension so the water can boil at a lower temperature. Hot water collects in the column that forms the geyser, slowly rising. As the hot water collects in the column, the pressure increases, eventually causing a certain portion of the water to become superheated. This water ultimately becomes steam, which rises and pushes the water above it out into the air. The geyser erupts.

Why is Geysir so well known? After travelers started to write about their experiences in Iceland in the 18th century, this spouting spring garnered considerable attention. The hot springs were thought to be one of the country's most impressive natural wonders, as Europeans had never seen anything like it. In the 19th century, a trip to Iceland was not complete without a stop at Geysir. Already there were signs of damage to the environment because of visits to the site, as clods of dirt and rocks were hurled into the geyser to make it erupt. Pictures of Geysir appeared in books, magazines and newspapers all over the world with the thinking that Geysir was a unique phenomenon, as Yellowstone's geysers were not discovered until 1870. It's thought that Geysir began erupting after a 17th century earthquake, but by 1910 it had stopped almost entirely. All throughout the 20th century there were various attempts to reawaken the spring, including digging a shunt into the base of the geyser's column (which today would be called environmental mutilation) to pump it full of soap for special occasions. And just when everyone thought it was all over, some powerful earthquakes in 2000 shook up the spring so that it still erupts to this day. It's not as active as it once was, but far from dead.

22

ÞINGVELLIR

What is it? The plains where Iceland's parliament, the Alþingi, was held every summer from 930 to the end of the 18th century. Now a national park on the UNESCO World Heritage List and an emblem of Alfred Wegener's theory of continental drift.

What's to see? No medieval historical sites in Iceland show any obvious impact from mankind. Þingvellir entered the nation's history at the establishment of the Alþingi in the 10th century, but you'll be hard pressed to see any signs of it. There are no buildings to see at Þingvellir besides a modern church and a house to match. Visitors are told of what happened at the site, but there's little to memorialize the history besides nature itself. The area is divided into a rift along the water and the plains along the river Öxará. Many of the rifts are impressive, but most visitors walk along the largest rift, Almannagjá, which used to gird off the ancient parliament. At the top of the rift is a lookout point with vistas over Þingvallavatn lake and the lava fields to the north and east. There's also a visitor centre with information on the basic geological elements behind the site.

Theory of continental drift. Many say that the rifts at Þingvellir are visible proof of German geologist Alfred Wegener's theory of continental drift, which today serves as the basis for our ideas about the origin of the continents. It's said that on top of the rift you're on the North American plate, while down at the river you're on the Eurasian plate. Unfortunately, this isn't quite right as the continental divide isn't really continuous, but broken up in various ways. But that doesn't mean that the Þingvellir rifts aren't the consequences of plate tectonics and volcanic activity. After all, Iceland is the largest visible portion of the Mid-Atlantic Ridge, which stretches from the Arctic Ocean to the South Pole and divides the North American and Eurasian continental plates.

The Deep End. On the plains to the east of the river are fissures in the lava field filled with water, connected to the other water systems in Þingvellir. The water in these fissures is ice cold and crystal clear. Not too long ago divers discovered an underwater world here, and pictures from the fissures have appeared all over including the cover of Time magazine. There are guided tours of the fissures for certified divers.

Twenty-two places you just can't miss when you come to Iceland. To see them all in one trip is no task for the faint of heart. This place is sparsely populated, and the enormity of nature dominates it wherever you look—although the people try to make themselves known at every opportunity parading out their culture and heritage for the last 1200 years the island has been settled. Even once you've seen these 22 places, you're still far from uncovering all of Iceland's secrets. But you will have come a little closer to understanding why this rock in the middle of the Atlantic Ocean is one of the most peculiar, yet more charming places in the world.